Earth Sky

AMOGHA

First Published in June 2021

ISBN: 978-93-5427-594-4

BLUEROSE PUBLISHERS
www.bluerosepublishers.com
info@bluerosepublishers.com
+91 8882 898 898

Cover Design:
Joshua Freitas

Typographic Design:
Namrata Saini

Distributed by: BlueRose, Amazon, Flipkart, Shopclues

To my beloved daughter, India.

Your smile lights up my universe.

Foreword

It is a chirpy night. I sit alone at the table, typing away on my computer, finishing off some pending blog edits at work, reflexively listening to the incessant chitter-chatter of the sleepless dad and daughter coming from inside the bedroom. Bedtime talks about incidents in school, dance performances, bygone holiday adventures, future expedition plans, vlogging themes, story ideas... The words flow non-stop, gushing on happily, through the ravines of imagination.

Suddenly in my head, a thought supervenes. A memory, tinted by the wistful colors of childhood, taking me a little back in time. In fact, years and years ago, in a different scene and time, this could have just been a little me at bedtime, breath held, wide-eyed... listening to the grand plans and enthralling lore of the sky and the earth narrated by my father. His tales always unfolded in a beautiful rhythm, just like poetry. Seems like it was only yesterday. How time flies!

For a moment I sit still... eyes closed. Set adrift on the sudden spate of memories the mind had unlocked. Frozen. Caught in the warp of time, having turned back to a page that the mind had bookmarked for eternity.

Poesy transcends space and time. And on its wings, perhaps we could soar higher towards embracing astonishing perspectives, making our short and ordinary sojourn on this planet enchantingly extraordinary. What an arid sphere our Earth would have been, without the mystery and magic of words. Through this book of poems, dear reader, I share my worlds, windows and words with you.

Amogha

About the Author

Amogha is a Communications & Branding professional, a Master's degree holder in Contemporary English Literature, a postgraduate in Marketing and a gypsy at heart. An unfinished affair with Journalism & a penchant for Cinematics lingers, which means the pursuit of knowledge shall continue.

When she is not writing, Amogha loves to read all the way to the moon and back, in a bid to comprehend outer space as well as inner space, lose herself in music, fiddle with photography and explore new places, cultures and cuisines. She lives in Pune, India with her husband & daughter.

Contents

Worlds

Worlds

'When was the last time
You looked up at the night sky, Surmi?'
She asked her curled up cat,
Who was pretending to be fast asleep
On an old crumpled cloth bag
Upon the floor of the boat,
Gently rocking in the rippling moonlight.

They both sat upon
The rocking little *vallom* tied to a post
Poking out of the tiny patch of lagoon
Outside their thatched home.
The kerosene lamp unexpectedly died down.
Fireflies shining like lit up emeralds
From within the thick hibiscus bushes
That cascaded
On to the waters behind them.

She asked again,
'When was the last time
You looked up at the night sky, Surmi,
Without any reason,
And suddenly wondered…
How you must be on a shining star too,
To some star-gazer
looking up at his sky,
From light years away
On some unknown sphere…'

Mystery Woman

Sometimes
Nature looks her best
When she dons the gown
Of a mystery woman,

Leading us
Into waters unknown...

Her glimpses of beauty
Leaving us
With dreams to be chased
And stories to be spun...

Brahm

An Ode to the Universe

Exploding into orbits of unending odysseys,
Conceived from the womb of nothingness,

Gravid with the curse of eternal unrest;
You traverse through unseen trails of timelessness.

The undercurrents of your consciousness
Shimmering 'neath an ocean of blackness

Break into countless whirlpools of lustrous light.
Myriads of iridescent circles,

Entwine inseparably in knots of radiant splendor
Living lives manifold, dying a million paltry deaths.

Showering your perpetual benevolence even upon
The tiniest sprouts that bud and flower from beneath the clay,

Tireless in your course of revolutions,
Unmindful of a destination, you wander
relentlessly…mystifyingly,

Armed at once, with the fury
Of Gods wielding lightning bolts

And the tenderness of a child holding a flickering lamp,
Tossing its unruly beams into the dark.

The nomad and the desert
Become one within you,

As you journey through infinite lights and shadows
In the vain quest for a beginning and an end.

Gaia

In a stupor lost, sits
The Architect of fates
Lost in the strange realms
Of her own design.
Old seeker of truths
Works her creased temple
Unsure of where from
Came the flaw.

Inane musings
Of the vacuous mind
Billows up in haze.
The ashen fog,
Clouding her gaze,
Dissolving the light,
Hides the rays.

Lines of worry
Criss-crossing the calm
Send forth ripples
Of pandemonium
Across the arid stretch of gray,
And she, now deposed
By her own constructs
Is old, blind and stray.

Sati

His tears burnt the heavens, where they fell.
It could have been her tender hands
Where the ashes now remained.

Clouds of dust arose from where
His bleeding feet fell in thunderfalls,
Eclipsing his mountain abode
From what remained of Celestium.

Every breath came like the storm unleashed,
Fury consuming the very ground
Where once they loved and lost.

And scorching fire was all that remained
Across the sky and the earth,
Lighting up her beautiful smile, etched in flames
Deep within His burning third eye.

The Mountain Epitaph

Ascending to the skies
In quest of a vantage view of mortality
Suffused in the spangled stardust,
Wreathed by the spiralling clouds

You tower tall, lone listener
To the dark designs of Celestium,
Cryptic, Filigreed across
The tapestry of the firmament.

Keeper of the sublime secrets
Hidden behind the pearly gates of paradise.
Mutely you writhe
Under the anguish of perceiving the unknown,

Unseen signs of Destiny,
Casting her shadow,
Menacing to snuff out
The despondent mortal flame,

Before it burns and crashes
To its own demise.
Before it maligns the pristine earth
With its macabre music.

Ending the enigma,
You shudder;
You tremble;
You rain

Stony tears of tremor,
Engraving in your heart,
An early epitaph
To an evanescent race.

To Dust

To think that birdsong & laughter,
Life's seemingly endless banter,
Feeling, emotion, thought & abstraction,
Lie, deceit, diversion & fabrication
Had a color & we never ever knew…

To think that success & failure,
Life's horde of inescapable allures,
Passion, will, patience & rapture,
Ambition, action, conscience & nature
Were all colored bright & we never ever knew…

To think that all we ever knew
Was that the sky was a spreading blue
And the earth, a diminishing green.
That we never ever knew
The interim of life was neither a shade of black nor white
But an all-pervading brown… as brown could ever have been.
As brown as dust could ever have been.

Identities

A transitory mortal
In pursuit of tranquility...
A million-faced plurality;
I am every soul
That seeks asylum in expectation.
I am every being who strives to stare
Through the veil of hope.

A placatory song
Sung to parched ears
A faceless reality;
I am Faith,
The defense to every question.
I am Conviction
The path to deliverance.

An illusory frame
Embodying the absolute...
A two-faced totality;
I am Existence,
The entirety of every passion.
I am Life
That seeks to engulf all...

Earth Sky

There was never a story,
But never a moment, dull or dreary
And there they were, always a little wary
The law of their universe, a little scary.

They could never ignore the alchemy,
Their bric-a-brac moments of conjury
That erupted like sparks of sorcery
Across their daily divine tapestry.

Gazes locked in eternal symmetry
Thoughts steeped in sacred poetry
Their borders were forever blurry
Entwined thoughts, ever so uncanny.

They never met,
And not even once, did fret
Over truths or tribulations,
They never did fidget,

For they lived, loved and longed deepest
Their yearnings,
In a silent tempest
That heaved within their hearts.

And at times, their dreams echoed
As thunder,
Lit up the firmament
Like lightning,

Fell down as magic spells of rain
That lightly kissed away,
Unbidden thoughts of pain
Ever so blithely drenching the twain,

The twain
That shall never meet.
The Sky and the Earth
An enthrallment that never fades.

Windows

Stallions

There were horses, four
They silently moved
Like ghosts upon the gravelly night
Silently chewing on the inky chill
Breathing in the dusty silence to their fill.

There were stallions, four
Once. All spirit and fire.
Full of power, grace and ire
Shaking their glorious manes at the envious sun
As they outstripped each other on the turf.

Treading a slower trail behind them
Now, their memories follow, unseen.
Of the green grass and the gunshots.
The smell of polished leather and wax
Of caresses by gentle hands.

The uproar of voices from the stands
Unwavering gazes from admiring eyes
Eager whispers in their ears
As they braced to race,
The looks of anticipation on each face.

They now move, like the spirits of the night
None to follow, none to guide
Their thoughts scudding across the scattered stars
Reflected in their eyes
As somewhere in the distance, the night-wind dies.

A Christmas Dream

We were lost in a Christmas dream together
In a lush green village at the tip of forever

Where paddy fields grew, and wild pollen blew
About in the golden firefly dusk, over the flowers.

There we stood as the church bells tolled.
Dressed up as kings. Patched clothes. Fake sword.

Eyeing balloons and pipes and people as they passed
Feeling hot, but proud in those robes, as they clapped.

Smiles and gazes paraded into the sunset
Without ever throwing a backward glance or a fret.

As the early moon ushered forth the first evening star
Across heaven's vibrant floor, so high afar.

Throwing lined eyelids wide open, I woke in haste
To look at you, at us, frolicking by that church gate.

Closed them again, hoping high, but in vain.
Yearning to get a glimpse of the faces I had seen.

As fond remembrances from that Christmas day of yore
Lapped gently upon the mind's weary shore.

Dreams are… I wondered, loving blanks in life's unfinished
rhyme.
Secret debts perhaps, that we never returned to Time.

Will I Ever?

Will I ever feel the same ache I felt as a child,
Upon seeing a fallen tree?

Ever feel the cold smooth velvety kiss of a river stone against
my face,
Hearing a gurgling river flow deep within?

Feel the rush of pride in showing off the biggest conch from
among the treasures,
Preciously gathered from the seashore?

Ever rejoice in baking a mud cake,
Blowing out stick candles, celebrating nothing?

Will I ever look at a waterfall and think there could be nothing
more beautiful in creation,
That can match its towering grandeur and deafening roar?

Will I ever leave behind my umbrella at home, intently,
Just to get drenched to the core in the falling rain?

Ever look at a bunch of everlasting flowers
And really believe they'd last forever?

Look at golden pupas 'neath the oleander leaves every day
Until they disappear into the world?

Will I ever think that I could be
All that I ever was?

Think that I could dream and re-live
The hundred and one lives I've lived as a child,

Will I ever?

The Perfect Day

Gossamer bales, diamonds and jade
Tintinnabulations of umpteen anklets
Swirling in the air.
Encircled by yards and yards
Of gold-bordered pastel white
She stands ornate beside
the delicately wrought mahogany mantelpiece.

The jasmine flowers on her hair-do,
A much too perfect white.
The paste on her face threatening to crack
To give it all away.
Her bangles make no sound
They seem to be in confederacy
With the entire conspiracy.
The perfect she-mannequin
Of the perfect day. She stands venting
All her patience into the ephemeral breath of The Day.

The expression unchanging, fixed.
Bold in the face of every flash.
Braving all ocular assaults
Displaying her price tag
On her crystal embedded silken bosom
Breathing in the perfumed air
Breathing in conversations like water

Every sound seems to gurgle around
Every word a cipher.
It all seems the same to her
A blinding wall of flashes
A sea of identical faces
With fixed pleased gazes, simulated smiles.

It still seems no different
Staring into the faceless groom
Hidden behind curtains of flowers.
The veil thrown upon destiny.
Blind eyes gazing into darkness.
A strained neck waiting to be strung.
Smiling, smiling, smiling
Away all the smiles of a lifetime
Till it wounds.

Paranoia

There are spinning cubes of diminishing ice now
Faded hues of my screwed-up face over a bitter lozenge
I'm no more the relic of my yesterdays
My past, now, I doth pity

I can taste the cancerous lemony smog in my first sip
Arraignments in the guise of innocuous banter.
The blinding fluorescent lights won't expose them
They send forth mere ghostly light.

The drumming of paranoid hearts all around,
I am at peace with the world at last?
Am I being awaited across the highway?
I run, ignoring the paranoid world. Ignoring myself…

Multicolored deaths speeding past from all directions
But I haven't got the time to die now.
Life awaits me across the highway
And I need to exist.

Moon Song

Tangled amidst the moonbeams
The never-ending moon-dust musings
Feeding on air and dreams
Spangled across space
Never too near, never far
Somewhere in the middle of nowhere
Suspended in the deep blue
Immersed in depths of thought
Deciding, and deciding hard
Upon dreams to disperse
Among forlorn windows.
Pallid eyelids unblinking
Wait for the crack of dawn,
The profound redness
Of an ever-evading absolution.
All that is heard is the sad chime
Of a dream broken loose.
Un-tethered and fleeing
Unseen into the darkness.

Windows

Forever lost in thoughts,
She has looked out of fleeting windows
All her life.
She felt it was always important to have the window open
Whenever she traveled,
This love often created small tensions
With the various clashing clans of motion-sick co-passengers
who preferred a sealed transit any day.

Nevertheless, she continued with her dreamy vigils
Through the open bus, train and cab windows on chilly
nights,
Letting the wind tangle her thoughts
And knot her hair into messy braids,
Returning home to hot cups of spiced pepper coffee
And scalding pots of herbs, steam and vapors,
To restore her wind-frozen senses for the next day's ride
And the next and the next...

Words

Ray of Hope

Teeth bared, eyes tapered to slits, spitting in rage,
Paced up and down the narrow confines,
An otter, grey.
Fraying the cord that bound its velvety neck to the cage.

Face fraught with disquiet, stood a frightened child petite,
Looking from the encircled pursuers' faces to the beast's.
The cogs of her mind working with all their might,
Deciding who could be the deadlier of the two.

The pursuers hooted and bellowed louder still, piercingly,
Happiness frothing forth, at the joy of conquering.
Their ancestors had been conquerors too. Unrelenting,
In the face of anguish mirrored in the eye of the captured.

Was it fear or ire in the eye of the beast?
The little one fathomed hard to comprehend.
A little voice within her mind breathed into her soul,
A silent prayer, a revelation in the face of her predicament.

The veil of night was drawn upon the landscape,
And, nature rested in serene repose, only to be broken
By a faint and feeble whimpering that arose from the cage.
A mysterious creaking of the door pricked the numb silence.

Fighting panic, a pair of little hands tugged
At the rusted lock of the cage,
Prying it wide open, running back in fear, not pausing to see
or think.
Amid a slight drizzle, darkness melted away into the
spreading dawn.

Morning brought with it more hooting and bellowing,
Vain and discontent faces contorted into grimaces.
And, a cloudless sunny sky, shone down onto an empty cage
Bathed in and out in the golden rays of hope.

Me Too

Evil is an effigy
Burnt to ashes every year
Scorning every unheard cry
Drowning every silent tear,
Its putrid breath raging on like hell fire
Eyes and limbs fervently groping minds
Probing skin and scars
Searching for what remains to be devoured of the soul.
The curse lives on, feeding on fears unsaid
As mute Goddesses live entangled
In austere entrapments
Revered, worshiped, desecrated, befouled
Time and again,
By faceless voices in the dark alleys of life
By murky whispers from rusty old telephones
By lustfully aloof eyes with lewd longing gazes
By blatant fleshly nakedness displayed at public places
By trust, by innocence, by the profane indifference
Deceptively clad in illusory robes of reverence,
Masking stories of horror...
Deceit and decadence
The evil breathes anew year after year
From effigy to effigy
From ashes to ashes
From now to ever
Mocking death, divinity,
And existence, forever.

Our Yellow Tennis Ball

It fell through time slowly, never reaching the end of the abyss.
It left my sight eons ago from your nimble grasp
Spinning madly into the dark eclipse of a nameless limbo,
Where I could see from now into then, when we had played
And laughed often, stranded on two sides of an invisible net
Amid stakes life had chosen to forgo.

You left in haste, with a heavy heart, never bidding adieu.
Spurning the million silent ovations; countless smiles and celebrations,
Unfurling unseen wings, waning into nothingness.

As your reflection melts fast unto oblivion's teardrop
As you fall asleep into a dreamless slumber
As you return to us as the wind, the sun and the rain,
A silent prayer... my beloved friend,
That the memories shall never wane.

Acquittals

Charmingly insane days of meaningful nothingness
Wane pale,
Withering the gauzy white flowers
Time guarded between their palms.

Puny souls that erred, that loved, that dreamt,
Exorcised into the limbo of eternal silences;
Lie entombed beside their own destroyed dreams
Deprived of deliverance and devotion.

Divinity works in mysterious ways...
Sometimes exonerating grave and ghastly sins,
But, blind to 'unforgivable' little mistakes
Whose puny sinners drown and choke
Endlessly in the waters of an unmindful Lethe,
Sans absolution.

9

I am capable of ruthless rancour.
I can break hearts, as I break wafer.

I can consume them without the remotest guilt.
I can then sleep in my own complacence.

I can digest them to the last beat mid slumber.
I can then dream that I am deliverer, guardian, liberator…

I can also see by-lanes as I walk upon the aisle of my trance
I can with ease ignore the muted angst I don't see.

I am malevolent by principle.
I am hideously egocentric to the deep dark depths.

I am the colossal shameless manifestation.
I am very very I.

The Drowning

Reading through
The walls I have built around
Me, you ogle into my soul
searching for woes
Eyes mirroring avarice,
You but a poor, flagrant
Villain in the making
Trembling, fumbling
Rattler of bones.

I, commander of the thunder
Harbinger of eternal rain,
Laugh the laughter of my life,
And as you, an asinine rodent
Run for shelter.
The thunder finds you
Pins you to the drenched ground
Soaking you in your own fear.
And you drown...

Pup

Beautifully he naps,
Snug as a bug in a rug
Smiling when the grass
Tickles his button nose
As the evening breeze
Plays host to his repose.
Lazily dreaming of all things wild
Unmindful of the thunder's
Deafening roar
Oblivious to the conspiracy
Among the rallying rain clouds
Underneath the sky,
Away from the crowds,
Tranquilly in the lap
Of a fleeting calm.
He sleeps.

Siesta

It's been a while since I'd been charmed
By the charm of a paperweight,
The coloured papers of an unknown spell of time
Tickling the chambers of reminiscence.
It's been a while since I'd been enthralled
By the mysterious scent of camphor and incense,
My mind glides on, tossing those bouquets
Of countless fragrances behind me,
Leaving a stream of fragrant remembrances in my wake.
The curls of smoke spiralling up from the joss,
Topsy-turvies into my mind,
Silhouetting into a strange shadow
Of the ringleted face of some old court arbiter,
In whose fist looms the thunderous giant gavel that mightily
falls,
Sealing fates, deafeningly piercing the stagnant sultry air,
Punctuating, puncturing & striking to a close, the somnolent
proceedings
Of my open-eyed noon siesta
On the drowsy bank waiting-chair.

You

My Other Half

My bubble of life, you surround me
Shading me from the hurtful haze
Curing me of despair
Soothing my bundle of nerves in your arms
Restoring me to my garrulous self.
Relentless.
Your choler unleashed
Makes me want to run and hide.
I take refuge
Somewhere within yourself
Frightened and lost I grope inside you
To redress my wrongs
I find you then, in me
Your arms speaking for you
I discover in you
The bearer of the halcyon light
Shining into my soul
And again & again we melt… timelessly…
Into the profound tranquil sea of life.

Words

She had often felt it was magic enough,
Just thinking about life on Earth.
Living upon the tiniest speck of a sphere,
Suspended in the ether of this endless universe.
Sipping on her strong tea,
Watching the incessant rain outside,
She let the pluviophile within her lap up
The musk,
The rising earthy scent
And the pitter-patter of rain music all around.
'Isn't the human mind a most baffling phenomenon,
Unlike anything at all', she thought,
As she soundlessly mouthed 'pluviophile'
To herself,
Sighing out a misty circle of breath
Onto the dewy windowpane...
She has never loved that word much,
Its verbal murkiness...
Yet...
To have bottled an entire array of aesthetic emotions
Into a single
Earthy word...
Enchanting!

Anecdotes

The smell of new books,
Of tea,

The musk of rain on summer earth,
The scent of fresh paint,

Of cinnamon,
The soothing green of sprouting buds.

Black ink, parchments,
Heart pulsing to the untamed beat of drums.

Frosted glass with spots of dancing lights
Falling from far amid the mist of mountain dusk,

Quiet reflections, by the roaring ocean
Pitter-patter of gray-blue monsoon nights.

Anecdotes of eloquent eyes, smiles that light up the world
Like the vibrant palette of an early morning sky.

Silences that speak aloud.
Mystiques of art that etch the trials and errors of an absurd
heart,

And all that has been, and will ever be dear...
Every breath, every beat, every act,

In the end...
A reminiscence for the last.

www.ingramcontent.com/pod-product-compliance
Lightning Source LLC
LaVergne TN
LVHW041755190726
843493LV00008B/2640